The Theory of Corporate Mind

Prateek Tandon

TO MY PARENTS,
Pramod & Meena Tandon,

Who dedicated their lives to their children,
And without whom none of my success would be possible.

Contents

Theory of Mind (ToM)

"The human mind is both the greatest weapon and the deadliest trap." – Robert Greene

(1)

In 1986, the US and the Soviet Union were on the verge of a historic agreement that would eliminate nuclear weapons in their entirety from the face of the earth. When Reagan and Gorbachev met in Iceland in October that year Reagan suggested that both superpowers agree to phasing out nuclear weapons altogether, to which Gorbachev replied "We can do that. We can eliminate them". Leading to a positive discussion thereon, both countries chalked out the details and agreed to all the conditions required to completely phase out their nuclear arsenal.

But the talks then stalled on the US's Strategic Defence Initiative (SDI), famously called the 'Star Wars' program, a space-based missile defense system under works. Reagan believed that SDI was essential even in a non-nuclear world and that the US should be allowed to test it in outer space. The provisional agreements were already drafted, and the discussion was in its last stage in the presence of Reagan, Gorbachev, and the entire diplomatic leadership from both the super-powers at a hotel suite in Reykjavik, Iceland. But Reagan decided to end the stalemate around SDI by abruptly walking out of the meeting. He was frustrated that the Soviets were not budging from their demand of confiding the SDI program to a laboratory rather than outer space for the next 10 years. The world that day lost an extraordinary opportunity to get rid of nuclear weapons altogether.

After a decade, one of the famous US diplomats Henry Kissinger tried revisiting this incident during a discussion with a retired soviet official, who was also an eyewitness to the entire episode [1]. Kissinger probed as to why were the Soviets so adamant about shelving the SDI program rather than proposing to separate it from other agreements and follow up on it at a later stage. It was then revealed that the Soviets were not exactly against the SDI program but rather they had no experts in the room guiding them on outer space nuclear strategies. Moreover, they also did not gauge the seriousness and importance that Reagan gave to this program.

Surprisingly, a case of perceived Soviet non-cooperation turned out to be a classic case of false perception. If only Reagan had the patience that day to understand the perspective behind Soviet conditions, and if only the Soviets attempted to understand Reagan's perspective better, humanity could have taken a historic step towards a world free from nuclear weapons. Understanding others from their perspectives is a natural cognitive ability of the human mind but, as seen from the case above, very often it turns out to be the hardest thing to do in a situation.

In the world of psychology, the basic human ability to understand another's perspective is called *Theory of Mind (ToM)*. It is a fundamental cognitive ability of the human brain that enables human beings to understand the mental states of others. It's described as a Theory because it is solely based on human behavior and actions. Several experiments have proven that ToM starts to develop in humans from a very early age and completely develops at the ages between 3 and 5.

Theory of Mind essentially enables the human brain to have the capability to identify the differences in perspectives of people around us. This is the reason why we see a depreciation of perspective thinking related abilities in people suffering from autism, schizophrenia, or attention deficit because all these mental states negatively affect ToM.

(2)

The Sally-Anne Test

Theory of Mind, when fully developed in a human brain makes it a generator of representations that can attribute beliefs, intentions, and knowledge to others and understand the causes of their behaviors. In a revolutionary experiment, conducted by British psychologists Simon Baron-Cohen, Uta Frith, and Alan M. Leslie in 1985, children are presented with a scenario involving two dolls, Sally and Anne.

Sally puts a marble into her basket and leaves the room. While she is away, Anne starts playing with the marble from Sally's basket and moves it to her basket. After describing this scenario, children are asked a few questions to test their ability of ToM: *where will Sally look for her marble when she comes back?*

Despite the knowledge that the marble has moved to Anne's basket, children who have developed ToM will answer that Sally will still think that the marble is in her basket. Named famously as the Sally-Anne test, this experiment initiated an avalanche of studies on understanding several aspects of the human brain, like empathy, perspective-taking, and related behaviors. The concept of ToM also became the basis of several studies in developmental and clinical psychology, giving birth to many early intervention programs for kids who show delays in understanding others' perspectives in their early years.

The development of ToM depends on the development of several parts of the human brain, majorly the Medial Prefrontal Cortex (PFC). This is the front part of the brain considered responsible for our thoughts and actions per our internal goals. Experiments and research based on neuroimaging techniques have shown that this part of the brain is also associated with social mimicry behavior, which explains why ToM and understanding of perspectives are the abilities emerging from mPFC.

The brain also houses two vital networks: the *Mentalizing Network* and the *Default Mode Network*, often called the "exploration network." Engaging in others' perspectives activates both these networks, likely due to the need to step beyond our mental boundaries to comprehend someone else's thoughts.

The *Mentalizing Network* comprises the temporoparietal junction, situated just above and behind the ear, and the dorsomedial prefrontal cortex, positioned behind the middle of the forehead. These areas are instrumental in understanding the thoughts, desires, needs, and priorities of others. Notably, research conducted by renowned neurologist Tania Singer's team in Germany has shown that the *Mentalizing Network* of the brain expands following nine months of exercises focused on perspectives.

This observation suggests that the mentalizing network functions akin to a muscle: its strength grows with consistent use. Consequently, regular involvement in understanding perspectives not only triggers specific brain regions but also fortifies the mentalizing network. This strengthened ability to understand others' perspectives may lead to enhanced capability that can be used to understand colleagues and managers in an office setup.

What are Perspectives?

*"Life is about perspective and how
you look at something…
ultimately, you have to zoom out."*

– Whitney Wolfe Herd

(3)

Perspective is the natural orientation of a person towards every situation in life, and this orientation stems from a person's beliefs, experiences, and context of the situation they are in. Perspective determines how motivated a person is to take certain actions in a situation. Everything in our social, professional, and personal environment is an outcome of the perspective that we have in life. In most cases, a person's perspective decides their companionship and social groups.

Perspective is one of the most interesting psychological concepts we have discovered about the human brain. Professionally, our perspectives are also responsible for decision-making and coordination with teams and it even impacts our overall productivity. As corporate employees, we must deal with many colleagues, departments, managers, and teams, each with a different perspective. It is crucial to swiftly navigate through these different perspectives while keeping our personal and professional goals in mind. This book describes several psychological hurdles that will come our way while trying to sail through the complexity of perspectives at our workplaces.

Several scientific studies have demonstrated the power of perception and its origins in the human brain. Perceptions in an adult are believed to be formed by a combination of natural human intelligence and learning from external experiences. The best example of a professional perspective gained through life experiences is 'an internship' or 'apprenticeship'. Students are advised to opt for internships early in their careers, not only to gain experience of how things work but also to be exposed to a new perspective which ultimately makes them a part of an industry. Understanding the perspectives, of others and our own, reveals the unwritten rules within the work culture of a corporate.

For example, using perspectives to learn strengths and weaknesses of team members or the real power equation within the team. This brings unparalleled clarity into what an employee should focus on to make themselves count. Charles Darwin, the most expert observer of nature ever in human history, spent several years on a ship as an unofficial "intern" observing people around him. Initially, for several months he was emotionally damaged and could not fit in with the strangers and the crew on board. But once he started attempts to observe and understand their perspectives, he was able to swiftly navigate through all the emotional and interpersonal issues, finally ending up being on a successful 5-year long voyage.

The ability to look at things and act based on our perspective is inculcated in a human from a very early age. However, research proves that the ability to understand others' perspectives inculcates from the age of two, powered by *Theory of Mind (ToM)*. There are also several ways that our brain uses perceptions for functioning in our daily lives. Studies have revealed that the human brain uses perceptions to quickly identify itself with an environment or group of people possessing similar psychological viewpoints.

In this process, the brain divides the world into "us and them", making a person cognitively favoring one group against another. In psychological terms, these are called "in-groups" and "out-groups".

(4)

In-groups, Out-groups, and Stereotyping

People with similar perspectives quickly come together and psychologically identify themselves as a social 'in-group', enticing a sense of belonging and closeness among each other. Others with different perspectives are psychologically distanced and considered as 'out-group' and often stereotyped as having a set of characteristics different from our own.

Throughout our lives we find ourselves associated with many *in-groups*, belonging to the same city, same school, or same profession. Corporate culture is the biggest hub of such perspective led closed in-groups: like the ones formed by frustrated employees, or by the ones who are in the boss's inner circle, or even by the ones who were awarded for their performance last year.

Classification into in-groups and out-groups is not a bad thing to do, as many studies referenced in this book will demonstrate. The problem starts when a common perception within closed in-groups starts percolating through the hierarchy of an organization in the form of stereotyping, which leads to biases and prejudiced behaviors towards out-groups.

Stereotyping influences a newcomer's initial perspective about a company, and it sticks with them for a long time. This is the worst trap an employee can fall into. This book will illustrate some of the major workplace biases that negatively influence our thought processes and hinder our cognitive *Theory of Mind (ToM)* abilities. Being aware of these biases lets us avoid falling into the trap of stereotyping and successfully navigate through a challenging corporate environment.

Not only does your perception of your teams and colleagues matter, but also their perception of you holds equal importance. One must, always, be consciously aware of their team's perception about themselves. This will tell you where you fit in the entire puzzle and how important, or significant, your contribution is to the team.

Theory of Corporate Mind (ToCM)

*"Your perspective on life comes from
the cage you were held captive in."*
~ *Shannon L. Alder*

(5)

The Sally-Anne test described earlier is a part of experiments to prove a psychological concept of False-Belief. Stemming from *ToM*, False Belief is the mental state where kids start developing abilities to realize that others may have a set of beliefs and viewpoints different than their own. This forms the basic stepping stone of understanding perspectives, and it is inculcated in a human at a young age and continues to grow with social experiences till adolescence. But like all the other things that come to us for free, we soon forget the importance of our abilities to mirror other people's viewpoint.

By adulthood, we do not consciously use our natural ability to analyze others' perspectives for personal or professional situations. Speaking from my own experience, I have seen many young candidates getting rejected in interviews because they sounded clueless in their answers. It's not that they did not give the right answers per their viewpoint, but they could not judge the question well as per the interviewer's perspective.

One of the motivations behind this book is an attempt to have our younger generation realize how lucky we are as humans to have the ability to take another human's perspective. It is strange that the cognitive ability that is one of the strongest suits in a human till adolescence suddenly seems to depreciate in adults entering the corporate world.

So, what happens in a corporate environment? For many, corporate setup is an overwhelming experience in terms of people interactions and working as a group. There are hierarchies and hidden power structures within the team which also must be understood carefully. Many tech corporates & startups now follow an advanced Agile structure of Tribes, Squads, Chapters, and Guilds, as first introduced by Spotify in 2012. This means that a mid-senior level corporate employee is interacting with four to five different teams and managers on average at any given time in a company. To survive and thrive in such a complex environment people must be aware of their cognitive skills to understand the perspectives of their team members and most importantly, their managers. But it's not that simple.

Over time, we develop several biases unknowingly in our minds which hinder us from completely capitalizing on taking perspectives. The entire exercise of understanding perceptions emerges from human evolution. In primitive times survival was crucial and hence all human cognitive abilities were shaped to prioritize survival in any situation. Analyzing other humans around us to identify them as a threat (or not) to survival was thus an important brain function at that time and continued through evolution. This survival instinct has made the human brain lazy and though it still analyses other people around us, but it ultimately seeks the shortest route to decision-making.

Several biases introduced in the modern world make it easier for the brain to quickly jump to conclusions about others. Stereotyping is one good example that influences our brain to make conclusions within seconds of how smart, intelligent, or educated a person is by quickly identifying him or her with an already perceived group of people. Similarly, others around us are also biased and pass a judgement about us without really understanding our perspective.

In such cases, the decision is quick but almost always wrong due to a lack of understanding of real perceptions in a situation, resulting in a high level of assumptions.

(6)

Biases Influencing Theory of Mind

Recalling here the earlier example of the 1986 failed nuclear treaty between the US and the Soviet Union. A stereotyped image of the Soviets as being uncooperative, through the decades of the Cold War, may have contributed to Reagan's frustration during the summit.

The human brain looks for the smallest datapoints, correct or not, to make up entire perceptions about people without any further efforts to understand the real perspectives. In a way, these psychological workplace biases in a corporate environment diminish our natural *'Theory of Mind'* (ToM) into a new way of thinking that I term as *Theory of Corporate Mind'* (ToCM).

Theory of Corporate Mind (**ToCM**) =
Theory of Mind (**ToM**) + *Workplace biases.*

A countless number of online and offline leadership courses aim to guide today's corporate leaders to adopt a fair and just management style. Even the senior and mid-level managers are coached to embrace empathy, patient listening, fair judgment, and perspective thinking in their day-to-day operations. But despite all the hours of coaching, consulting, TED talks and other resources good bosses still remain a rare commodity.

Ultimately, the onus falls on the employees to fend for themselves and avoid the pitfalls of psychological biases at the workplace. In the forthcoming sections, we will understand some of the major workplace biases that impact our *Theory of Mind (ToM)* abilities.

The best way to counter these biases is a two-step process: *'Know it'* and *'Control it'*. This book attempts to make the reader take the first step and be aware of the biases they are dealing with in their offices. The second step is out of the scope of this release and will be covered in a separate book.

Egocentric Bias

"God can't fill you when you are already full of yourself."
— Max Lucado

(7)

IKEA, the famous Swedish company renowned for its flat-pack, self-assembly furniture caters to one of the strongest psychological biases of human nature: *Egocentric bias*. In 2009 three behavioural economists Michael Norton, Daniel Mochon, and Dan Ariely conducted an experiment that involved participants assembling IKEA furniture. Participants were given IKEA boxes containing disassembled furniture and were asked to put the pieces together.

After completing the task, they were asked to evaluate the value of the furniture they assembled against a similar pre-assembled furniture. The researchers found that participants consistently valued the furniture they assembled themselves more highly than the pre-assembled versions, even though the assembled ones were mostly imperfect or required improvements.

This experiment reiterates the significant influence of *egocentric bias* in our lives and shows how humans are biased to overvalue anything they have put efforts into, irrespective of factual realities and the quality of the end-result. This bias occurs when people rely too heavily on self-perception of their abilities and traits, often overestimating their abilities, contrary to facts.

Egocentric bias tends to mislead individuals to interpret the world from their subjective perspective, often overestimating the importance of their own opinions and beliefs while underestimating the viewpoints of others. This cognitive bias significantly influences interpersonal relationships, decision-making, and the interpretation of events.

A very real-life example can be found almost always at social gatherings or during office gossip sessions. There will always be someone who must interrupt to tell a better story about the same experience that somebody else is talking about. Don't you wonder if this interrupter is even listening to himself, let alone others? Well, they are listening to themselves more than they should. They believe their experience stands out to the extent that others' experiences are not worth their time.

The study of egocentric bias can be traced back to the early works of psychologists and philosophers, who observed how individuals often perceived the world through their subjective lens. However, the formal recognition of this cognitive bias gained momentum in the 20th century when psychologists began conducting empirical studies to understand the psychological mechanisms behind egocentric thinking.

One classic experiment demonstrating this is the *Anchoring effect*. Participants asked to estimate a numerical value tend to be influenced by an initial, often arbitrary, piece of information presented to them (the anchor). This initial number serves as a reference point, leading participants to adjust their estimates insufficiently away from the anchor, showcasing their egocentric tendency to rely on provided information, even when irrelevant or incorrect. The anchor, even if it's a random number or unrelated fact, serves as a reference point for decision-making. The anchor has a lasting influence as even when people recognize that the anchor is irrelevant, their judgments are still affected by it.

Egocentric bias permeates various aspects of daily office life, affecting interpersonal relationships, workplace dynamics, and professional attitudes. The most common mistake we make under the influence of egocentric bias is to consider our understanding as the gospel truth. Consider the case when we are assigned to support a new project that is already established and running successfully. Our first step will be to understand the established processes, system protocols, and overall design so that we can support its functioning better.

However, often it happens that we gain some of the knowledge and assume the rest. This causes problems at a later stage when our assumptions trigger an incorrect diagnosis or cause a major disaster. We should always put our knowledge and understanding in writing and take others' feedback on it. This allows us to take different perspectives on our understanding of the new system and it also counters any assumptions that we have made from an egocentric point of view.

(8)

Counter-attack Strategies

Misjudgment of situations born out of egocentric bias can impede effective communication, build wrong self-perceptions, and strain relationships. Especially for employees working in client-facing roles, egocentric bias can lead to a big gap in perspectives between them and the client. Speaking in technical jargon, which is understood only by our colleagues within the organization, is the most egocentric conversation it can ever get on client calls.

Translating technicalities into a business language that a client understands is a major part of client-facing jobs. Understanding client's perspective plays a major role in accomplishing this translation. If we are very egocentric and focus more on our processes and jargons than what the client understands, then it soon becomes a frustrating conversation without any productive results in sight.

Egocentric bias continues to shape perceptions, interactions, and decisions in the office environment.

Often, we may dismiss valuable ideas from others or rush to conclusions, assuming our perspectives to be superior, thereby hindering proper understanding of the situation. Salary negotiation is one popular victim of *egocentric bias*, through 'anchoring', in the corporate world. Any salary figures discussed initially, by any party, could influence the final negotiated salary because the initial figure gets stuck in the candidate's mind from the beginning. Thereafter, any small amount on top of that initial "anchor" feels like a good deal for the candidate.

We can attempt to understand this bias and then consciously attempt to mitigate it by following some steps:

- First and foremost, being consciously aware of the anchoring effect can help us recognize when it's influencing our decisions.

- At this point, to balance the bias, we can introduce multiple anchors by deliberately considering multiple sources of information. Like, talking to colleagues and understanding what's going on in the project that is outside our purview or understanding the perspective of a colleague who has been having a hard time maintaining quality of work.

- Finally, concluding after analyzing multiple sources of information can bring us to a more realistic anchor blended with different perspectives.

As an example, we may sometimes feel a need to bring some concern about ourselves to the notice of our boss. From our viewpoint, it may be a very important point to raise, but before actually raising it we should analyze and counter any egocentric bias inflating its importance.

- ✓ How does this concern impact our productivity? Is this the right time to raise this?

- ✓ Is the boss currently occupied with something else more important in the project than dealing with our situation?

- ✓ Is there any other information we need to collect before discussing the situation with the boss?

These may be some questions we can ask ourselves to decide the best course of action. Our situation may seem a top priority for us but may not be the same for the boss to take it on priority, and that's something we need to analyse.

By recognizing and mitigating egocentric tendencies, individuals can navigate the corridors of the corporate world by understanding the real priorities and perspectives of a group. Mitigation of egocentric bias helps us in creating a more harmonious work environment, where diverse perspectives are valued and respected.

Confirmation bias

"Confirmation bias is the most effective way to go on living a lie." ~ Criss Jami

(9)

In retrospect, we now know that there were very early signs of a huge market bubble that led to the financial crash of 2008. A few hedge fund managers like Steve Eisman, Michael Burry, and John Paulson stood out and were able to predict the crash well before it happened. However, most of the industry analysts were not able to see the warning signs, not because they did not have the correct data to look at but because they probably didn't want to look at something that goes against the prevalent notion of a healthy market.

This is a classic example of a powerful cognitive bias, that influences the way we consume information and make decisions. It is called *Confirmation Bias* which is a deeply ingrained tendency that leads us to seek, interpret, and remember information that aligns with our existing beliefs while disregarding or downplaying any contradicting evidence.

Its roots lie in our brain's quest for cognitive efficiency; we tend to process information in a way that preserves our preconceived notions and reduces mental effort. However, this cognitive shortcut often leads to distorted perceptions and judgments. Ventral Striatum, in the outermost layer of the brain, is activated when humans encounter information that confirms their beliefs. It reinforces the existing neural pathways associated with our beliefs and strengthens the confirmation bias by making us feel rewarded for confirming our beliefs. Contrary to this, the Amygdala, located in the temporal lobe plays a role in emotional processing and can trigger emotional responses when confronted with conflicting information.

If contradictory data challenges deeply held beliefs, the amygdala might trigger a defensive emotional response, reinforcing the avoidance of contradictory information. Usually, any suggestions or feedback from our colleagues or superiors, that do not align with our viewpoint, can trigger an emotional reaction automatically. But this is where our ability to consciously understand others' perspectives helps us to remain focused on the situation and dig further to frame an appropriate response rather than letting *confirmation bias* trigger a natural defensive reaction to the situation.

Raymond Nickerson, a renowned cognitive psychologist, conducted significant research [6] that presented glaring insights into the depths of confirmation bias. In his whitepaper, he concluded, *"If one were to attempt to identify a single problematic aspect of human reasoning that deserves attention above all others, the confirmation bias would have to be among the candidates for consideration."*

Nickerson's findings revealed how individuals tend to interpret information to align with their preconceived notions which results in challenges to unbiased objective thinking, reasoning, and decision-making. Through his experiments, he found that people tend to actively seek out evidence that supports their hypothesis while neglecting potentially valuable information that challenges their beliefs.

The research demonstrated that individuals are often unaware of this biased processing of information, emphasizing the deeply ingrained and automatic nature of confirmation bias in human cognition. Due to confirmation bias, we tend to lose out on giving our attention to minute details that may be important but do not appease our beliefs or state of mind. A conversation with colleagues and stakeholders is not always full of positive vibes, and mitigating the confirmation bias will ensure that we do not miss learning from the best out of everything thrown at us during a typical workday.

(10)

Confirmation Bias in Action

Often our notion of how our job should look like or becoming comfortable at a routine job limits our thoughts and vision. Any changes to job responsibilities or daily tasks, assigned by our managers, may then feel like something new outside the realms of our sense of confirmation and may feel like a disruption. This may result in anxiety, and we may end up rejecting a new work or task assigned to us in the organization, irrespective of the long-term benefits it might bring.

The ultimate loss of opportunity by not thinking beyond our beliefs and being in our comfort zone, driven by *confirmation bias*, may cost us dearly in our careers. Maybe the manager is trying to test our capabilities beyond the line of work that we are already doing. Or maybe they have a bigger plan for us, and the new task is just a small preparatory part of it? These are some of the questions we should try answering to counter the inbuilt *confirmation bias,* before taking a decision.

There is an interesting experiment, called the Wason Selection Task, that proves that we naturally look at the information at hand for confirmation and give almost no importance to other evident facts present right in front of us. In this experiment, conducted in the 1960s, participants were given a set of cards, each with a letter on one side and a number on the other.

The rule to be tested was: "If a card has a vowel on one side, then it must have an even number on the other side." Participants were shown four cards with different letters and numbers, and their task was to determine which cards needed to be turned over to test the rule. Most participants selected cards that, if they had a vowel on one side, would confirm the given rule. For instance, participants typically chose the card with a vowel on one side and an even number on the other, intending to confirm the rule, neglecting the importance of testing cards that could potentially disprove the rule. Wason's experiment highlighted how people tend to confirm, not falsify, their hypotheses.

Here is another perspective on confirmation bias. The realization that we can navigate any situation by understanding others' confirmation bias comes in handy many times, such as in hiring interviews. An interview, in simple terms, is an exercise driven by an interviewer's confirmation bias. It is an attempt by a company's representatives to understand if a candidate socially and technically fits into the organization and role they are looking to fill.

Almost all the time a confirmation that on social parameters a candidate is similar to their existing employees drives the outcome, considering the technical expectations are met. Conscious attempt at understanding perspective during an interview can help a candidate frame answers in a way that satisfies interviewers' confirmation bias.

Pluralistic ignorance

"There is no darkness - but ignorance."
- William Shakespeare

(11)

In Africa, funerals stand as pivotal life events. They've evolved into expensive social gatherings with ornate caskets, custom attire, and lavish feasts, forming a significant expense in many African nations. A 2009 economic study revealed that "honorable" funerals in South Africa from 2003 to 2005 cost around $400 to $500, accounting for about 40% of the average yearly household spending [7]. This imposes a considerable financial strain on grieving families already dealing with emotional vulnerability.

Surveys indicate that when asked privately, a substantial number of people in African countries do not support such lavish spending on funerals. Nonetheless, they persist in adhering to this cultural norm, assuming it's supported by the majority, thereby perpetuating the tradition. This is the same case as the fat expenditures on weddings in Indian subcontinent culture. Even though most people individually reject a particular norm, they end up embracing it publicly because they falsely believe that others support it. This example can be extrapolated to an office environment where employees do not counter their superiors or colleagues during discussions, even though privately they have a different viewpoint.

If this has ever happened to you in office, then you are not alone. The human brain is a survival machine and always keeps a watch on situations of group rejection which is why we choose to not speak our minds out in conflict situations. This condition arises from a cognitive bias called *Pluralistic Ignorance*. In social psychology, *pluralistic ignorance* refers to the situation in which the majority of individuals in a group privately reject a norm, but mistakenly assume that most others accept it. This collective misperception profoundly affects our behavior, perpetuating norms in the workplace that nobody truly believes in.

In one of the most famous experiments on this topic, conducted in 1968 called **the Smoke-Filled Room Study,** researchers staged a situation where participants were placed in a room filled with smoke. When participants were alone, they quickly reported the smoke. However, in the presence of confederates who were instructed to ignore the smoke, participants hesitated to report the emergency, assuming their perception was incorrect due to the inaction of others. In another experiment called the **Drinking Norms Study,** college students were found to have overestimated perceptions of the amount of alcohol their peers consumed, leading to an escalation of drinking norms throughout the campus. Despite individual reservations about excessive drinking, the misperception of others' behavior fuelled a collective acceptance of heavy drinking, showcasing pluralistic ignorance's influence. It arises from the interplay of individual beliefs and societal pressures, creating a situation where people publicly adhere to norms they privately reject, due to a mistaken perception of others' beliefs.

(12)

Netflix Rules

The phenomenon of *Pluralistic Ignorance* thrives in situations where social conformity is high, and the fear of social ostracism outweighs the urge to express personal opinions. What can be a better playing field for this than a usual office workplace that demands segregation based on hierarchy, seniority, and performance? Pluralistic ignorance makes people mistakenly believe that everyone else holds a different opinion than their own. As a result, most people in a group may go along with a view they do not agree with, because they incorrectly think that most other people in the group agree with it, especially when the outcomes are not their responsibility. However, this is not the correct approach to take at a workplace.

At Netflix, famous for its it's productivity-driven workplace culture, it is akin to being disloyal to the company if employees fail to speak up when they disagree with a colleague, manager, or even the leadership. Reed Hastings, ex-CEO of Netflix, believes that an employee's approval of pluralistic ignorance and conforming with certain beliefs in a workplace only makes him or her one amongst the mediocre corporate heard and dampens their natural ability to understand other perspectives.

There must be a fine balancing act between not falling for pluralistic ignorance and calling out on somebody in front of others. In the process of speaking our minds out, we must be careful that it doesn't lead to hurting egos and burning bridges with colleagues and managers. So, our choice of words here is always crucial. It's not always that people go along with the others in a group and keep mum only in the cases of negative feedback to somebody. It's also often the case with positive feedback as well.

(13)

The case with positive feedback

Consider a scenario where a colleague shares a brilliant out-of-box solution to a problem or a new project that the team is handling. Even though individually the team members might agree that the idea is brilliant, as a group they may not share their affirmation or positive feedback. The right approach for dealing with such situations without falling for pluralistic ignorance is to prepare a ground for understanding different perspectives. A step-by-step approach should work here.

- The first step should be to carefully float your perspective about the situation. If it's a negative callout we should be careful and use words that are more positive but still convey the point. Note that we should not just conclusively pass a statement in this first step. This should only be a step to reveal our thoughts and introduce the group to our thought process. Like saying *"Do you think we should do a deeper analysis into this before concluding?"*

- The next step is to understand the perspective of the group based on the discussion that comes out of the first step. If our thought is taken positively, we should move towards a conclusion right there.

- If we sense a reluctance for further action in the group, then our approach should be more individualistic. We should then identify the key stakeholders related to the situation and understand their perceptions one-on-one by reaching out to them individually.

In many workplaces, emphasis is on teamwork and collaboration, which creates an unspoken norm where individuals are expected to excel quietly, without seeking acknowledgment or recognition. This norm fosters a culture of pluralistic ignorance, where employees privately celebrate their achievements or grapple with challenges but publicly conform to the silent consensus of downplaying personal performance.

We must tread carefully to not underplay our achievements at work, and at the same time to not overestimate them under the influence of ego-centric bias. It all comes down to how much impact our "achievements" had on the goals and priorities of our stakeholders, and how we present it to our leadership. If we accurately understand our bosses and project goals from their perspectives, then we can create a story around our contribution to showcase the maximum impact it had on those goals.

Moreover, it is very common to not talk about the mental stress and long work hours with our managers, because we think that it will make us look bad as nobody else in the team is talking about it. As corporate employees, we must be very open about our limits of working under stress that doesn't impact our health. Even though during team calls nobody admits, we should not hesitate to raise the point of long work hours beyond the stipulated time affecting our health.

Altogether, it is important to identify the environment of pluralistic ignorance and then address it by clearly understanding the reasons behind it, like what's the different viewpoints preventing team members from speaking up. Conformity can lead to missed opportunities for professional growth, as well as hinder the overall productivity and creativity within organizations.

Privilege of Knowledge

"Those who have the privilege to know have the duty to act, and in that action are the seeds of new knowledge." ~ Albert Einstein

(14)

Psychologist Walter Mischel from Stanford conducted an experiment in 1972, called the *Stanford Marshmallow Experiment*, which proved to be a well-known study into human psychology from various aspects. As part of this experiment preschool children were placed in a room with a single marshmallow on a table. Each child was given a choice: they could eat the marshmallow immediately or if they waited for 15 minutes, they would receive a second marshmallow. The experimenter then left the room, leaving the child alone with the marshmallow.

Children who exercised patience often had better academic outcomes. But on looking at the results from another perspective it was revealed that children from disadvantaged backgrounds often could not exercise restraint. This was because they lacked the privilege of knowledge about delayed gratification's importance in life. They knew only how to utilize what in the present was right in front of them and so they ended up eating the marshmallow. This is called *Privilege of Knowledge* where a person's perspective is shaped based on the level of knowledge they are exposed to. Under the influence of *privilege of knowledge* people, unaware of others' experiences and perspectives, might struggle to relate to different viewpoints.

Though a simple fact, it's often a big realization that while knowledge is universally valued not everyone has equal access to it. Socioeconomic factors, disparities in educational opportunities, systemic biases, and different career paths create barriers, leaving many individuals without access to the wealth of information and insights that probably most of us take for granted. This is the reason why to make sense of decisions taken by our managers we should first acknowledge that both parties have different perspectives based on their levels of privilege to knowledge. It may happen that a new boss may have switched industries in their career recently, and so their decisions are influenced by the limited knowledge they have about their new organization.

Certainly, they'll come up the knowledge curve in time, but in the meanwhile, we need to understand their perspective and take action accordingly rather than complaining and whining about it, or even getting frustrated.

Beyond the surface, the privilege of knowledge's intricate layers encompasses disparities in education, access to information, cognitive skills, and societal perceptions. An awareness of the existence of different levels of privilege of knowledge at a workplace can make our lives easier. The privilege bias works both ways. It may be a possibility that our managers themselves are unknowingly influenced by a higher privilege of knowledge bias while interacting with us. Of course, due to their hierarchical position, they will be in the know of a lot more information than us, but that should not become problematic in the form of unrealistic expectations from us.

It is crucial to identify the presence of such bias in our interactions with the boss and understand the perspective to address this bias with a positive approach. Often, after being in an industry for some time it is assumed that we are aware of some prevalent processes, standards, and jargons. However, every organization has its own version of standards and processes it follows internally.

A privilege of knowledge bias can result in our managers having an incorrect perception, that being experienced in the industry, we are aware of all these processes as per their version of it. This may result in conflicts at a later stage, if not dealt with initially. It is a great first step to identify and address such perceptions so that both parties are on the same page of expectations.

(15)

Are you Well-informed?

It should always be our goal to be on the higher side of the *privilege of the knowledge* spectrum, especially on the tasks that are assigned to us in the workplace. Often, influenced by bias, employees are given half-baked information about a task without realizing the existence of crucial knowledge gaps that can impact our progress. Several experiments conducted by psychologists have proven that being "well-informed" has a remarkable difference in our decision-making abilities, to the extent of being a crucial deciding factor for our success or failure.

In these experiments, participants are divided into two groups: one group is given detailed information about a complex decision-making scenario, making them well-informed, while the other group receives limited or no information, making them uninformed. Both groups are then asked to make decisions related to a scenario. The study observes that the well-informed group's decisions add value and are respected more. The "well-informed" decisions are more likely to achieve their desired goals as well.

To achieve such results despite the influence of *privilege of knowledge* bias, we must ask as many questions as we can intending to be satisfactorily "well-informed" about a task before starting on it. This will reveal various aspects, perceptions, and valuable information that can come in handy for proper decision-making or troubleshooting and will also ensure minimum assumptions influenced by the bias.

Privilege of Knowledge bias can also sometimes lead to extreme behaviours from people in leadership positions. Managers possessing extensive knowledge, irrespective of its relevancy, might inadvertently try to exert power over us. This dynamic can affect the balance of respect and influence in boss-employee relationships. It requires a foundational understanding of our managers' experiences, perspectives, and knowledge disparities that can avoid resulting in a lack of understanding and compassion in relationship.

The actor-observer hypothesis

*"We are very good lawyers for our own mistakes,
and very good judges for the mistakes of others"*

~ Paulo Coelho

(16)

On April 23, 1985, Coca-Cola launched its new Coke formula in the market. The company discontinued its original formula, replacing it entirely with the new, sweeter version. Not much later, this went down in history as the most epic marketing failures ever. The public rejected the new Coke and the company had to face a swift backlash from its loyal customers for discontinuing the original Coke. A week later, it was only sensible for the company to announce the return of the original Coke as "Coke Classic" which finally helped them keep the market share intact.

In retrospect, when asked about this epic failure Coca-Cola executives attributed the decision to reformulate to situational factors such as market research data and the need to adapt to changing consumer preferences.

Contrary to their analysis, consumers interpreted this change as a reflection of Coca-Cola's lack of understanding of its heritage and the emotional connection people had with the brand. But how can the same situation have two different root causes? Mostly because people tend to explain their behaviors with situational causes and others' behavior with personal causes.

In this case study, Coca-Cola executives blamed external situational factors like changing consumer behavior and market research. The die-hard fans of the original Coke blamed this on the lack of understanding customer perspective by the company. In this situation Coca-Cola is an 'actor' and the loyal customers are 'observers' making this a classic example of another psychological bias called *the Actor-Observer Hypothesis*. At its core, the actor-observer hypothesis explores the disparities in attributions made by individuals concerning their behavior versus the behavior of others.

This is not a new scenario at a corporate workplace, especially during an year-end retrospective analysis or 360-degree feedback activity when employees often try to attribute their mistakes to external situations, but their managers attribute it to dispositional factors like employee's individual personality traits, temperament, and commitment. No matter what we do we cannot eliminate this bias from our manager's mind. All we can do is respond in a way that counters the bias to the maximum, keeping our image and perception intact in front of the team.

Studies have shown that positive feedback in a social or workplace setup releases Oxytocin, or 'happy hormones', which makes us happy, strengthens social bonds, and enhances feelings of trust and connection between individuals. But at the same time, if the feedback is negative or if someone calls out our mistakes in front of our tribe then the Amygdala, the most primitive part of our brain, gets activated. It triggers a defensive and even emotional or panicky response. The easiest route, hence, our brain takes is to find a scapegoat which is mostly an external factor.

However, this makes things worse. As soon as we blame external situations it risks our reputation at the workplace. Maybe it's a mistake genuinely caused by factors outside our control, but as soon we swipe the facts under the carpet and immediately conclude that it's because of external factors, it becomes hard for people to believe.

(17)

Don't let them judge!

The Actor-Observer bias suggests that people tend to attribute their actions to external factors or situational circumstances while attributing the actions of others to internal factors or personal traits. Thus, we can safely assume that in such scenarios our boss, influenced by actor-observer bias, will be associating even the smallest mistakes with our deeper (in)capabilities. To counter this, right at the outset we should accept that the situation could have been handled better.

Clearing this at the beginning avoids a logjam and bitter arguments and brings the stakeholders to the table for a deeper analysis before conclusive attribution. Now, we should use this as a chance to understand stakeholder perspectives and analyze the real impact of the mistakes that occurred. Our final response should be to calmly lay out facts, including the dependencies on external factors that influenced our behaviours, coupled with the intensity of impact it has caused on the broader organization goals and priorities. This kind of measured and undisturbed response addresses the issue at hand and at the same time works to maintain the boss's trust in our abilities.

In a notable experiment, two distinguished Professors of social psychology, Jones and Nisbett [8] presented participants with a debate. One participant (the actor) argued a specific viewpoint, while another participant (the observer) watched the debate. After the debate, observers tended to attribute the actor's arguments to their personality traits, while actors attributed their arguments to the debate topic, demonstrating the actor-observer bias in attributions.

Taking a cue from this, we should be careful in jumping to conclusions about decisions taken by managers and overall leadership. Influenced by the bias we may attribute any unfavourable results to our boss's personality traits. But a deeper understanding of perspectives may reveal facts to the contrary. The profound impact of actor-observer bias could make us judgmental in our opinion and hinder our ability to understand people's perspectives, take shortcuts, and use stereotypes to conclude any situation.

Set-up-to-fail Syndrome

"Bosses create their own poor performers."

~ *Harvard Business Review*

(18)

Why does an employee perform badly? Most bosses would answer that by attributing it to personality traits of the employee like weak skills, inability to prioritize properly, poor communication, and lack of motivation. But is it always the employee's fault? Or does the buck stop with the boss? Most often the boss and employees are unknowingly caught in a bias called *Set-up-to-fail syndrome*, which creates and reinforces a dynamic between them that essentially sets up perceived underperformers to fail.

The *set-up-to-fail syndrome* influences a scenario in which employees perceived to be performing unsatisfactorily live down to the low expectations their bosses have for them.

The result is that the employee often ends up with declining overall performance and productivity, even though they have the traits and knowledge to perform better. It can start with even a small trigger that raises doubts about an employee's performance in the boss's mind. It can be anything from missing a deadline, or unsatisfactory quality of the work, and the bias kicks in. Often the reason is not even specific. It may be the case that the employee was transferred to a new project or department with a not-so-great recommendation.

As at the start of any new relationship, in the boss-employee scenario, even small events at the beginning can make a lasting impression. Once a boss begins to worry that one of his subordinate's performances is not up to par, he will start giving that employee more time and attention than others, micromanaging each and everything, demanding answers even on the aspects of daily operations that are working fine. More documentation, more micromanagement, and more personal focus, all because the boss seems convinced that without his watchful intervention, the employee will flounder and mismanage something or the other. This is akin to parents giving more attention to the kid they perceive as the least talented or underperforming among the others.

Though the boss's intentions are positive and are aimed at improving the employee's performance, without a proper understanding of this perception by the employee it becomes a recipe for his continued poor performance and drastic failure. The increase in supervision by the boss is interpreted by the employee as a sign of a lack of confidence and trust in the leadership. This causes the employee to doubt his or her own capabilities and thinking, and gradually they lose motivation to be more productive at work. They reckon whatever they do boss will question it and ask for more documentation or ultimately do it himself. This chain of thought diminishes the motivation to work and turns into an avalanche of falling productivity, quality, and performance of the employee.

The boss, on the other hand, interprets the employee's behavior as a withdrawal and becomes further convinced that he is indeed a poor performer. After all, the employee does not seem to be contributing to the organization with their full energy and ideas. To make things right, the boss increases supervision even further to the levels of watching, questioning, and micromanaging everything. Eventually, the employee gives up on being able to contribute anything at work.

The boss and the employee then settle into a routine of cordial relationship with a satisfactory performance, avoiding any clashes or conflicts. This is a point-of-no-return and no matter what the employee does from here they can rarely make an impact or change the perception in front of the boss. In the worst-case scenario, the employee may even go into complete inaction and will start consuming more and more of the boss's time. Finally, a call is made to let go of the employee, considering they haven't quit already.

(19)

The Harvard Study

Harvard Business Review came across a classic real-life example during their study on *Set-up-to-fail syndrome*. Steven, a new boss, joined a manufacturing company and had a quality manager Jeffrey reporting to him. In the initial days of their relationship Steven, the boss, asked Jeffrey to write up an analysis of significant incidents in the quality control process. Steven intended to have failures documented to learn and improve from them and to understand the processes in detail for his own learning. This unsettled Jeffrey who was perplexed as to why he should spend time in writing about the processes that he already has experience in and understands well.

A clear gap in perspectives here led Jeffrey to believe that this was an act of interference from Steven, and he did not spend time and energy on the expected documentation. As a result, Steven suspected that Jeffrey was neither really a good performer nor a proactive manager.

Unfortunately, further interactions between them turned more into forceful attempts from Steven to make Jeffrey do the reports, which were quietly met by his passive resistance. As we can imagine, this spiraled into Steven spending more and more time trying to micromanage Jeffrey's daily operations ultimately frustrating him to the point that he was on the verge of quitting when the HBR's team met him for the study.

The most interesting aspect of set-up-to-fail syndrome is that like a vicious circle, it is self-fulfilling and self-reinforcing. Ironically, it is self-fulfilling because a boss's actions encourage the very behavior that is expected from weak performers. And when the boss's low expectations are fulfilled by his subordinates, it triggers more of the same behavior from him.

It goes on and on and with each action and reaction, the relationship goes spiraling downwards. The onus here is on the employee to ensure that they identify the existence of a *set-up-to-fail syndrome* in their relationship with the boss by consciously taking the boss's perception into account. Simply reacting to the boss's requests and demands without understanding the perception behind them can cause things at the office to spiral out of hand.

In-group, out-group bias

"Why be a star when you can make a constellation?"
~ Mariam Kaba

(20)

In 1724 Benjamin Franklin ended up in London and found himself a job in a printing company. He had good experience in the printing industry and had the right skills for the job he had landed himself in. Everything seemed to be going fine for the initial couple of weeks and he got along well with his colleagues. Soon enough he encountered a strange British custom at the workplace: five times a day his colleagues would take a break to drink a pint of beer. Supposedly, this kept them motivated and more productive at work. But Benjamin was different. He did not like to drink during work hours but as a part of the workplace he was expected to contribute to a weekly 'beer fund'.

He let his colleagues know about his thoughts and refused to pay, and they accepted his decision politely. But that is when strange things started to happen to him at work: mistakes kept popping up in texts he had already proofread, or some new error for which he was blamed. Gradually it became clear to him that this was a silent retribution for not contributing to the 'beer fund'. Finally, the problems disappeared once he agreed to join others in the tradition and dish out money from his hard-earned salary.

In a perfect world, this could be categorized as an injustice towards Benjamin, but in the realistic world we live in, this is a reality. People around us are driven by a sense of belonging, constantly identifying themselves with a group of people possessing visible similarities. By refusing to join colleagues in a "useless" tradition Benjamin may have considered himself to be a reformer, but from his colleague's perspective, he proved himself unfit to be a part of their inner circle. For a human brain, the world is divided into simple 'us' and 'them' and in a workplace, it is very important to tread this line carefully.

Categorizing the world into 'us' and 'them' is a way for our brain to function effectively. Labeling is something that we all do to make things easy for us by providing our brains with a readymade guide for interpreting events for interpersonal interaction. With this categorical distinction, our brain can swiftly decide how to behave when interacting with close relatives or friends, as opposed to an acquaintance or stranger.

This categorization into 'us' and 'them' is defined as *in-group* and *out-group* respectively in psychological terms.

At a workplace, *in-group* and *out-group* classification comes into play during the quick decision-making by managers about who should be assigned what tasks. Several studies reveal that most bosses are consciously aware of this phenomenon but consider it as part of being more effective and productive rather than a bias. Up to 90% of all bosses treat some subordinates as though they are part of an *in-group*, while they categorize others as an *out-group*. Members of the in-group are in the circle of trusted associates and therefore receive more expressions of confidence from their bosses.

(21)

Relationship with the boss

The relationship with the boss for the *'in-group'* subordinates is much cordial with mutual trust and reciprocal influence. Members of the *out-group*, on the other hand, are regarded more as hired hands and are managed in a more formal, less personal way, with more emphasis on rules, policies, and authority. This is where it becomes a bias and works against many employees who do not take notice of this phenomenon superimposing on the relationship with their boss.

It is important to consciously understand the existence of *in-group out-group bias* in our workplace environment. From a boss's perspective, having made up his mind about a subordinate's capabilities and motivation, he is likely to give more important and strategic tasks to subordinates that identify with his *in-group*. This is not a new spectacle in corporate offices. Several cases of *in-group out-group* bias result in junior colleagues being assigned more responsibilities bypassing and undermining senior folks in the team.

Bosses may find nothing wrong with it because they are looking at this through their biased perspective about the capabilities of a few subordinates in the team. At the end of the day, they want to get the work done and it doesn't matter if it goes through the proper chain of command or not. In the process, the reputation and trust of some hard-working and capable subordinates get damaged, even without doing anything wrong.

This is where we should learn to "read our boss's mind" to get clarity on what defines an *in-group* and *out-group* for him. Usually, analyzing differences in the boss's behavior with us and other colleagues will lay out a clear picture of which group we belong to.

As human behavior dictates, bosses tend to have less patience while interacting with *out-group* folks. This would lead to a perceived lack of confidence, criticism, disapproval, and even arguments with the employee. At this point, we should not get disappointed or enraged or shut down trying to defend ourselves.

Rather, we should try to investigate more to understand the perception behind such behavior from the boss. Some key questions should help:

- ✓ What are the performance levels and quality of delivery that a boss expects?

- ✓ How proactive, punctual, or process-oriented one should be to be safe from the out-group bias?

- ✓ What defines a good performance in his or her dictionary?

The onus is on the employee to frame and ask these questions to the boss. There may be initial resistance in getting clues towards answering these questions, but a conscious step-by-step approach (discussed later in this book) may help counter and navigate through the rough waters of the boss's out-group bias.

Pratfall effect

*"Our little pebble of poor performance helps to start,
or to sustain, an avalanche."*

~ Neal A. Maxwell

(22)

During a 2008 presidential campaign speech, Barack Obama made a notable gaffe while speaking about the number of states in the US. He said, "I've now been in 57 states; I think one left to go". The United States has only 50 states and thus this was a mistake. But as we now know, this mistake certainly did not affect his campaign significantly.

During the same presidential race, Sarah Palin was running for vice-president as a Republican candidate. In one of the live interviews during the campaign when asked about her reading habits she struggled to recall even a single magazine or newspaper that she read regularly. She met with fierce criticism throughout the media because of this incident, to the extent of even calling her gaffe as the rise of "anti-intellectualism" in the US elections. It impacted her campaign and experts say that it may have cost the votes of many who were still undecided or were new Republicans.

But a question arises: despite his gaffe how Obama managed to pull it off with respect to public perception, but Sarah Palin couldn't? Considering both sides have similar campaign expertise, was there anything else at play here? Barack Obama from the beginning came across as a mature, calm & responsible candidate. However, Sarah Palin was not perceived as a serious candidate or as somebody who was an extraordinary performer. These perceptions from their very early days in the campaign decided the way public opinion would behave whenever they commit small or genuine mistakes in the future.

While Obama's mistake was seen as a part and parcel of a stressful campaign, Sarah's gaffe proved to solidify the not-so-great performer perception she already had in the eyes of the public. In fact, according to observers, Obama's small mistakes during the campaign trail made him more likable among the people. But at the same time, every small mistake by Sarah immediately reflected a decline in her popularity numbers. This is due to a psychological phenomenon called the *Pratfall Effect*.

Coined by psychologist Elliot Aronson in 1966, this effect reveals a fascinating aspect of human behavior where interpersonal appeal and perceptions change after an individual makes a mistake, depending on the individual's earlier perceived competence. People tend to find average-seeming individuals become less likable and highly competent individuals become more likable even if they commit the same mistake. This phenomenon practically doubles down on the *Set-up-to-fail syndrome* as after committing even the smallest of a mistake it may reduce the likeability of an already perceived low performer in the eyes of the boss.

Elliot Aronson, an American psychology professor at Harvard University, along with his colleagues designed an experiment where participants listened to recordings of a person answering a quiz. This quiz was a staged interview conducted with an actor, who played the role of either an unrealistically knowledgeable individual (answering correctly 92% of the time) or a mediocre one (answering correctly only 30% of the time). The participants heard these interviews, which were followed by the high-performing actor admitting to a successful high school career, and the low-performing actor describing an average academic life. In some cases, the actors even spilled coffee to test the effect of a mistake on people's perception.

The experiment's findings revealed that participants rated the knowledgeable individual who made a mistake as more attractive, while the mediocre performers experienced decreased perceived attractiveness. Now, in a workplace environment, this will apply even to false perceptions a boss has of a subordinate's performance. If after understanding our boss's perspective it is revealed that he doesn't consider us as a high performer, we should be extra careful of making even small mistakes. It adds some pressure on us, but being consciously aware of this phenomenon helps us while framing a counter-response to any mistakes we might commit.

(23)

Perceptions at Workplace

Interestingly, *the Pratfall Effect* drastically impacts the perspectives of how a workplace should be perceived by average and high-performance employees. An employee perceived as a high performer in the eyes of the boss seems to have ample scope for mistakes. Consecutive studies on the Pratfall effect have given us an understanding that when good performers commit small mistakes it makes them more relatable and practical in front of people, which in turn makes them more likable.

However, in the case of mediocre employees, the same mistakes are considered as a sign of vindication by the boss on the perceived low performance of the employee. An employee must understand how his actions & mistakes will be perceived by the boss. If we already know that we are not among the mediocre performers, it may be beneficial for us to not aim for perfection every time.

There is a common question often asked in interviews: "What are your weaknesses?" Everyone has weaknesses but we always try to answer this question with as much positivity as possible. We are worried about letting our real weaknesses be highlighted during the interview process. But considering the impact of *the*

Pratfall Effect, this question should now make more sense. Here letting the interviewer get a glimpse of our real weakness may work in our favour and make us more relatable and likable to the interviewer. This is a positive angle of *the Pratfall Effect.*

Similar usability of this psychological phenomenon is used in the entertainment industry through Bloopers where all the actors, each portraying a character on-screen flawlessly, show their off-screen mistakes and imperfections of the entire production. This makes them more relatable and works as a great marketing strategy.

Along the same lines, we can use the *Pratfall Effect* to our advantage by understanding the perspective of an interviewer. The intention of an interviewer asking about our weaknesses is to know the version of us that is more relatable. We should consider that question in our minds as *"What in our performance could surprise the interviewer after we join the company?"*

Keep in mind, that posing as a flawless candidate for a job opening may rule out the possibility that the interviewer will be surprised by our good performance after joining the organization. Thus, the only event that may surprise him could be a weakness or a repeat of a mistake that we may have committed in our career earlier. Letting some of the smaller flaws known during an interview may help in becoming the perfect candidate for the job.

The pratfall effect will also impact our psychology at the workplace. We must be careful and conscious of our actions and behavior to be not influenced in the wrong direction due to this bias. Take a scenario when we have a new boss or colleague joining the company who is just adjusting to the new environment and ends up committing a mistake. We should not let this create a negative perception of them in our minds else this could later result in unpleasant interactions and a toxic culture at the workplace.

We must be watchful of the *Pratfall Effect*, especially in the case of our interaction with the known mediocre or low performers in the office. Their mistakes should be judged based on the level of impact. We cannot ignore the high-impact mistakes, but at the same time cannot let smaller ones instigate bias against them. A better analysis on a case-to-case basis should help counter the biases of *the Pratfall Effect.*

Horn Effect

"Eliminate as many judgments of others in your thoughts as possible." ~ Wayne W. Dyer

(24)

In 2017 a group of researchers from Japan conducted a study on the impact of 'First Impressions' on tourists visiting the city of Kyoto. The first impressions like "Typically Japanese," "Felt history," and "Felt tradition" were found to have lower satisfaction levels for tourists than "Doubtful" and "Mysterious". Tourists also revealed that they would want to go to other sightseeing spots in the area only if they felt the first impression had a positive effect on their satisfaction levels. Overall, the study concluded that first impressions had long-lasting effects on people's minds to the extent of influencing and motivating them to take certain actions.

It would, therefore, not be an exaggeration if the word *first impression'* is described as *'an initial perception that is hard to eradicate from people's mind'* and it naturally creeps into corporate culture causing a strong bias at our workplaces. Within a matter of time, bosses and colleagues can assume and pass judgments based on looks, dressing sense communication skills, etc., which will stick to perceptions of our other traits for a long time.

This cognitive bias is called *The Halo Effect* which is the psychological term to describe situations when initial impressions lead an individual to assume that if someone possesses positive qualities in one area, they are likely to excel in other areas as well. More than often an overall impression of a person influences how we feel and think about their character, abilities, and other traits. A negative effect of this bias called *The Horn Effect* can lead our colleagues and managers to negatively estimate our other traits based on a single disliked aspect of our personality.

First impressions influence future behavior and cooperation, and this is something that we cannot eliminate around us. We cannot avoid being judged by others and no matter how hard we try to have a perfect image for ourselves, our first impressions will always be misleading. *The Halo* and *Horn* biases are deeply instilled in human psychology, and we have no control over them. They help the human brain to connect the dots using the facts it knows about others, or in shorter words: to assume the unknowns. For example, when reading a series of numbers like this – 0, 10, 20, 30, 50, 60, 70 – what comes to our mind is the missing 40. The brain connects the dots here and rightly assumes that there should be a 40 in between.

(25)

The First Impression Experiment

Solomon Asch, a Polish pioneer in social psychology, experimented [9] in the 1940s specifically in the context of impression formation in the human brain. In his experiment, participants were given a brief description of a person. The only difference in the descriptions was whether the person was described as "warm" or "cold." Participants were then asked to rate the individual on various personality traits. Asch found that the person described as "warm" was consistently rated more positively across a range of traits, such as kindness, generosity, and sincerity, compared to the person described as "cold."

People seemed to extrapolate the warmth trait to assume other positive qualities about the person, showcasing the pervasive impact of the initial impression. Similarly, while making decisions in the office, a boss assumes several unknown traits and capabilities based on the overall impression of a subordinate. This links future projects, assignments, and responsibilities to the initial impression that we make, and thus the responsibility lies with us to identify and fill the gaps in our boss's misleading perceptions about us.

As John Gribbin, the famous British science author, says in his cult-classic work 'Deep Simplicity':

"Some systems … are very sensitive to their starting conditions, so that a tiny difference in the initial 'push' you give them causes a big difference in where they end up"

It is always better to act early than to regret later. To be on the safer side, we must always assume that this bias plays a crucial role at every step of our career: when we join a new company, a new project, or a new team. Always try to put forth a great first impression in front of the boss but at the same time, always assume that your attempt of a good first impression wasn't enough. Keep probing about your overall impression on the team and with your boss.

But what should our first impressions be like? People often make the mistake of trying desperately hard to appear the way they perceive themselves. But this is a mistake. We must understand the perspectives of the boss and team members to find what is expected from us. A clear understanding of team members' perspectives will help us find our perceived place and need in the team. Our first impressions should fit this perceived role.

For example, a senior analyst has joined a new team, but a project manager has left at the same time. During the period when a new Project Manager (PM) takes over, the senior analyst realizes that the boss is expecting somebody to take over the PM's role temporarily. In his conversations with the boss, he starts mentioning his previous experience and practical knowledge as a PM. He even starts taking initiative and performing as a PM for some smaller projects. This creates a good impression of the analyst as being someone capable and willing to wear multiple hats in his role. When the time comes who do you think will be considered from within the team to fill the PM role temporarily or permanently?

It is crucial to understand the right gap in terms of what the team requires so that we can align our skills and the impressions we create in the team.

There is no theory which defines a good or bad first impression. However, a very famous area of scientific study, Chaos theory, explores the underlying patterns that are highly sensitive to initial conditions. A very interesting concept of the Chaos Theory is called the *Butterfly Effect* wherein a small change in starting conditions can lead to vastly different outcomes even to the extent that a small butterfly flapping its wings could, hypothetically, cause a typhoon.

There is no fixed path or pattern to people's careers in the corporate world and thus we can never surely know how big a jump-start our slight push on initial impressions can bring to our careers.

Loss Aversion

"If we could be freed from our aversion to loss, our whole outlook on risk would change."
~ Alan Hirsch

(26)

Humans are social animals with a great survival instinct. Many habits, biases, cognitive abilities, and survival traits have developed through the evolution of the human species over thousands of years. The human brain has learned from the primitive years that if one only has enough to survive then an increase in resources will be helpful but a decrease in those same resources could be fatal. This perspective has been consequential in how we still see opportunities at hand.

A modern human brain still gives more importance to avoiding loss than to gaining something of the same value. Consequently, people are driven more by the prospect of losing something of value than by the prospect of gaining it. This is called *Loss Aversion*. In a workplace, this could lead to a reluctance against new opportunities, new people, and even changes in processes and policies.

A study published in the Journal of Applied Psychology [10] in 2014 revealed that decision-making is highly influenced by *Loss Aversion* in workplaces. In this study, employees were presented with hypothetical case studies involving failing projects and were asked about their decision to either continue or close the project due to sunken costs.

The conclusions revealed that people were more likely to continue investing resources in a failing project. Even when the project's future success was doubtful, participants were hesitant to withdraw due to the perceived loss associated with prior investments. This is where loss aversion impacts our decision-making in a workplace environment. Fear of the loss of what we have at hand coupled with the uncertainty of the unknown that a new process, assignment, or role will bring, often creates bias in our decision-making capability.

Several studies conducted on how humans make decisions have revealed that losses cause a greater emotional impact on an individual than does an equivalent amount of gain. But we should not let emotions get in the way of how we perceive changes happening at our workplaces. A boss may look at a process from a third person's perspective and find flaws in it. To make things better he might propose to change the process altogether and it may be a complex transition to do. Our first reaction cannot be skepticism driven by *Loss Aversion* which contributes to a preference for the status quo.

When faced with a decision that involves potential gains or losses, individuals may perceive maintaining the current state (status quo) as a way to avoid potential losses. This is because any change from the status quo is often perceived as a potential loss, even if the change could potentially result in gains. This is a very well-documented phenomenon demonstrated in a 2005 study where people refused to give up money for vouchers that can be exchanged for chocolate, perceiving it as a potential loss. Even though the value of cash and vouchers are technically the same, people perceive giving up cash as a loss.

(27)

The Prospect Theory

When facing situations triggering *Loss* Aversion at a workplace, we need to carefully follow a few steps to respond in an unbiased manner and make the right decision. With a conscious understanding of the situation we are dealing with, we can avoid falling for loss aversion. *Prospect Theory*, formulated in 1979 and further developed in 1992 by cognitive and mathematical psychologist Amos Tversky, gives good insights into how decision-making works and how we can counter loss aversion. It asserts that decisions are made through a two-stage process that narrows down the most important details to be considered for decision-making: *The editing Phase* and *Evaluation Phase*.

Editing Phase: This is the information-gathering phase where after evaluating the situation people decide on which information is relevant for decision-making in the next phase. This is the phase where we need to be very careful about what information we prioritize as important. Influenced by *Loss Aversion* we may take mental shortcuts to register the information inclining in favour of status-quo, because that's only what we want to hear. But if we try to understand the deeper perspective behind the change, we may be able to prioritize a balanced set of information both for and against the change. Frame questions for the boss and ask the details of the change and why the leadership thinks it's required. Try to gather the probable impacts proposed changes are likely to have on us and other stakeholders.

This phase is crucial because a careful understanding of perspective in this phase can avoid the introduction of biases that can emerge later in the decision-making process. If we do not consider the right perspective and do not evaluate the situation based on balanced facts, we may end up making incorrect decisions leading to lost opportunities. You may never know why the boss is pushing for the introduction of a new process even though the current processes are working just fine. Maybe they want to train people on a set of new tools that will help in future projects.

This kind of information can only be dug up by understanding deeper perspectives behind the situation. The first natural thoughts that come to an employee's mind in the face of new processes or policy changes are about job security, status, or benefits. But we must train ourselves to look and think beyond the obvious to be able to navigate through changes at the workplace swiftly.

Evaluation Phase: Based on the assessments made in the editing phase, people make their decisions in this stage. Probabilities of outcomes are weighed in, and actions are taken based on the perceived desirability of each outcome. Prospect theory establishes that people tend to be highly risk-averse when the stakes are high but highly risk-accepted when the stakes are low. In other words, final decisions in such situations are highly focused on minimizing losses rather than maximizing expected gains.

So, it is safe to assume that these decisions are biased by *Loss* Aversion and not necessarily based on rational calculations. Re-examining possible outcomes based on the results of the previous step can help reduce the impact of this cognitive bias. The addition of other people's opinions through understanding perspectives can lead to thinking in terms of the value of expected outcomes rather than in terms of gain and loss. Lastly, do not use the present conditions as a reference point because the outcomes are to be considered for a time in the future. This can help reduce our loss aversion bias while making decisions in the workplace.

Illusionary correlation

"Correlation does not imply causation"
~ David Hume

(28)

Negative and stressful events in our lives remain easily memorable and unfortunately influence our mindset more than pleasant memories. Picture yourself visiting New York City for the first time. Chances are that a negative encounter might stick in your memory for a long time. Like an unpleasant interaction with a restaurant waiter or someone behaving rudely on the subway. Surprisingly, these isolated incidents might occupy a mere fraction of your overall time in New York yet hold considerable weight in shaping your perception of the entire experience.

The reason is that negative incidents directly affect the Amygdala region of the human brain and leave an emotional mark that is easy to recall for any future reference. Psychological studies have proven that the human brain tends to overestimate the importance of events that are easier to remember, as opposed to the events that we have trouble recalling. So, since the inconvenience faced during the New York trip sits at the back of your mind and is easily recallable, your recommendation to anybody visiting NYC may revolve around these incidents.

As a human tendency, we are most likely to create a strong relationship between two things that are weakly related or not related at all, as in this case where in all probability we will link the negative incidents to the overall New York trip. This is called *Illusory Correlation* which causes us to see an association between two variables (events, actions, ideas, etc.) even when they aren't strongly associated. Think about *the illusionary correlation* influencing our workplaces. Any negative outcomes, no matter how small, will be recalled easily and mistakenly correlated to our performance at the workplace. Several leadership or internal organization courses make managers aware of such biases to avoid illusionary correlation but for the sake of our careers, we cannot rely on the boss and wait for him to do the right thing. We must be conscious of the fact that there will be mistakes and our superiors will be influenced by this bias to easily recall and associate these mistakes with our overall performance.

Illusionary correlation in a boss-employee relationship is a result of less visibility and not being on the same page. Several times during discussions we may have a perception that certain actions or questions from the boss are judgmental or undermine our work, but mostly this thought process is correlating two completely unrelated events. Unless this *illusionary perception* is cleared by understanding the boss better, it will continue to demotivate us at the workplace. A unique study done by European business researchers in 2010, found an interesting case of *illusionary correlation*. The study focused on how perceived golfing performance was positively related to CEO compensation. This is to say, CEOs who play golf well make more money than those who don't— an average of nearly 15% more, the study found.

The general perception related to this statistic was that performance on the golf course was a cue for corporate performance. People associate a CEO's record on the golf course with how good they are at their job. However, researchers found this correlation between performances to be not true. It is, in fact, negatively correlated. The only thing the golf course was found to contribute was a great social network which seemed to catapult CEO's salaries irrespective of their performance in the job. So, the association between golf performance and corporate performance turned out to be an *illusory correlation*.

(29)

The Buck Stops Here

As with many other cognitive biases, *illusionary correlation* also has its origins in human evolution. The human brain recalls negative memories quickly probably because those who are more attuned to bad things would have been more likely to survive threats in the primitive world. Survival requires urgent attention to possible bad outcomes but less urgent to good ones. But this bias being passed on through generations of mankind's evolution becomes a problem in a workplace environment. Professor Amabile of Harvard Business School conducted an experiment [11] with the help of corporate employees and collected around 12,000 diary entries about their thoughts on relationships with their bosses.

She found that the negative effect of a setback at work was more than twice as strong as the positive effect of an event that signaled progress. The power of a setback to increase frustration is over three times as strong as the power of progress to decrease frustration. If managers or bosses know this, then they should be acutely aware of the impact they have when they fail to recognize the importance to employees of making progress on meaningful work. But the buck stops with the employees to identify and understand if they have fallen victim to *illusionary correlation* bias from their bosses.

Professor Nass from Stanford University puts forward an interesting theory [12] to identify illusionary correlation behavior in a workplace. He declares that we tend to see people who say negative things as smarter than those who are positive. Thus, at a workplace people are more likely to give greater weight to critical reviews. The right way to identify an illusionary correlation in a boss's behavior is to analyze the level of critical behavior. If the criticisms are high and bordering on toxicity the boss is most likely to have fallen for the bias.

Researchers have found that illusory correlations tend to occur mostly under conditions when participants are not personally involved. In other words, bosses are most susceptible to falling for illusionary correlation when they do not have a good understanding of our work, personality, and other social parameters. This results in lower motivation to deeply understand our perspective and rather take shortcuts to form opinions about us based on completely unrelated factors.

We must ensure that understanding each other's perspectives doesn't fall between the cracks in our relationships with the boss. Even if initiated by an employee, perspective thinking ends up giving better visibility to both parties about each other and counters any illusions.

Contrast and Assimilation Effect

"The human understanding when it has once adopted an opinion ... draws all things else to support and agree with it." ~ Francis Bacon

(30)

Victor Lustig, the most famous American conman during the early 20th century, once "sold" the Eiffel Tower to a French businessman. He pretended to be a French bureaucrat and created for himself a repository of fake government collaterals including the official French government seal. In 1925, a newspaper article illustrated how the French government was finding it hard to maintain the Eiffel Tower in a period of a struggling economy. Taking a cue from this, Lustig presented himself in front of a group of French Businessmen as the government official assigned to "offload" the Eiffel Tower to save the government from the burden of its maintenance.

The best trick that helped him pull off the scam was to make himself look even more natural in his role by asking for a bribe, which was an unwritten norm expected from government officials at that time. Finally, he successfully "sold" the Eiffel Tower and escaped to Austria. But a very significant learning from this incident was how people believed him to be a government official. Lustig's act of asking for a bribe made him highly believable because people usually look for just enough information on others to fit them into their pre-existing notions. As soon as Lustig asked for a bribe he won the trust as a real government employee and the rest unknowns about his behavior were assumed automatically.

A similar process happens at the workplace when we get a new manager or colleague. We try to analyze them on the standards set in our minds from our previous experiences. As a natural tendency, we try to quickly contrast or liken them with our older bosses or colleagues. This is called *the Contrast and Assimilation Effect* and it leaves very little room for forming correct opinions based on understanding perceptions. The *assimilation and contrast effect* is a cognitive bias that distorts our perception of something when we compare it to something else, by *reducing* or *increasing* the apparent differences between them respectively.

The assimilation effect makes people appear more similar to one another whereas, the contrast effect makes people appear different than they are. For example, the assimilation effect can influence people who have seen someone acting in a hostile manner, and that causes them to view other people's behavior as more hostile than they would otherwise feel. Imagine if influenced by this bias we settle for building a wrong perception of our boss after comparing him or her with one of our previous bosses. Our behavior and relationship with the boss are in danger of going highly off-track once the wrong perception settles in. This can even go to the extent of predicting future events in our relationship with the boss.

(31)

Individual Beliefs and Conversations

Let us continue the previous example of an old and new boss. Norbert Schwarz, from the Institute for Social Research at the University of Michigan, proposes [13] that a human brain creates a mental representation of a target (the new boss) and of a standard level to which the target is compared (the previous boss). Both representations are based on the information at hand during a specific situation.

So even though we know less about the new boss and more about our previous boss, the human brain still ends up comparing both to pass judgment even in the face of a clear lack of information.

Schwarz's research finds that information used to contrast or assimilate depends on several personal factors:

- Individuals' beliefs, considering if the information was recalled by some irrelevant influence, and

- Conversational norms that influenced the perceived relevance of information.

Individual beliefs are the most critical factor because the direction of thought process is decided by the fact that as a person, we look for similarities or dissimilarities between the target and the standard. Searching for similarities between a standard and a target leads to their coming closer in our minds, whereas searching for dissimilarities leads to differences of opinion with them.

If our beliefs can be controlled to keep us away from passing judgments, at-least before we have enough data points to form a thoughtful opinion, then we could be at a better place in our workplace relationship with the new boss. This is also where we can use understanding of perceptions alive by using it as a technique to gather relevant information to counter the bias.

It is safe to assume that the contrast and assimilate effect will influence the decisions on our performance evaluations as well. If we can compare the boss with our previous managers, then the same can also happen to us. Boss can, and will, compare us with his previous subordinates. The result could be that the boss templatizes our performance to the standard of a previous employee, in the process, magnifying our fault lines and ignoring our strengths. Hence, the identification of this bias in our interactions with the boss, by understanding his or her perspective, is very crucial.

From the information-gathering conversations, it is important to precipitate an understanding of how the boss approaches decision-making and intends to evaluate our performance. Implementing structured decision-making processes can help reduce the impact of biases. This might involve using standardized evaluation criteria for performance assessments or any other equivalent structured processes that can make it harder for biases to seep into decision-making.

Perspective-Taking to Counter Biases

"एकं सद् विप्रा बहुधा वदन्ति"
ekaṁ sad viprā bahudhā vadanti

Meaning: "Reality is one,
though wise men speak of it variously."

~ Rigveda, one of the oldest Hindu scriptures.

(32)

It is ironic that despite having most of our lives full of social and professional interactions, it's still hard for us as humans to understand the world from another human being's perspective. Neurologically, we are a very self-centred species. Studies have revealed that in most situations, our minds gravitate toward our own or known perspectives.

Despite the basic *Theory of Mind (ToM)* that enables the human brain to mirror others' thought processes to some extent, understanding people's perspectives in any situation is a skill that needs to be consciously triggered and practiced. A famous parable of blind men and elephants found in Buddhist and Hindu texts shows how people around us have different perspectives which are important to understand the big picture.

The story of *Blind Men and Elephants* describes a group of blind men who encounter an elephant and end up interpreting the animal based on the part each man touched. One man likened the elephant to a snake when he touched its trunk, while another compared it to a fan, having felt its ear. Each person's description varied, from a tree-trunk-like pillar to a wall, or a rope, based solely on the part they examined.

This narrative vividly portrays how individual perspectives, limited by personal experiences and sensory input, shape our understanding of reality. Understanding the intricacies of human perceptions depends solely on the angle of observation or the facet explored. Thus, it becomes very essential that while being in a social or professional setup, we consciously realize the perspective of others to react accordingly.

This process is called *Perspective-taking* and if consciously done it utilizes natural *Theory of Mind (ToM)* capabilities to help us understand other's perspective and counter psychological biases, including the workplaces biases described earlier.

(33)

Perspective-taking vs. Empathy

Perspective-taking is the skill of understanding another person's psychological point of view, beliefs, or actions in a situation. It is like *"putting ourselves in others' shoes"* and understanding the world from their perspective. This should not be confused with Empathy, which involves understanding another person's feelings regarding a situation.

Often, Empathy and Perspective-taking are used interchangeably. But that's not the correct representation of these two different skills. Empathy is when we try to feel what others feel in a situation, but perspective-taking is when we try to understand where the others are coming from and why do they feel like they do. A real-life example of perspective-taking comes from a famous FBI hostage negotiator Chris Voss. In Haiti, back in the 90s, Chris negotiated several kidnapping incidents which unusually used to surge at the start of every week. By talking and listening to several kidnappers over months, Chris could not only empathize with their situation but could also understand their perspective. Due to high unemployment and poverty rates in the 90s, Haiti's youth had taken to illegal routes of money-making, and this was something that Chris empathized with.

However, they were not professional kidnappers and from their perspectives, they just wanted to have money to enjoy the weekend and survive the coming week. This was the reason that most of the kidnappings happened at the start of the week and were aimed at getting money by Friday so that it could be spent lavishly during the weekend. Thereafter, Chris tweaked his strategy and aimed at dragging negotiations as much as possible during the week. In the end, when the weekend was near, kidnappers would agree to even small amounts of ransom, sometimes as low as $3000, to just close the deal and get away for the weekend.

Empathy is about understanding the surface-level emotions of people, and *perspective-taking* involves delving deeper and understanding the underlying reasons and motivations driving their actions and requests. This comprehensive understanding empowers us to counter workplace biases and devise creative solutions to achieve our goals while also addressing the core needs and concerns of all others around us.

(34)

Basic Steps of Perspective-taking

Perspective-taking is a vast subject in psychology and the entire topic is much beyond the scope of this book. The author here has attempted to guide readers on several cognitive biases that distract a human brain from effectively respecting perspectives of others at a workplace.

However, for a brief introduction, below are the two basic steps that should be followed to understand someone's perspective:

- *Information gathering*— to learn more about the person,

- *Inferential or reasoning*— based on the gathered information develop conjectures about a person's thoughts, motivations, and perceptions of the situation.

Like detectives alternating between collecting clues and formulating hypotheses, individuals often oscillate between the above two primary steps of understanding perspectives: *(a) gathering information to understand the person better* and *(b) making inferences to develop assumptions about their thoughts, emotions, and motivations in a situation.*

We might think it's better to get all the details about someone before guessing their perceptions, but interestingly these two steps go together. New information can help us guess what someone thinks. And when we guess, we might need more info to check if we're right, starting the cycle again.

McKinsey, the distinguished US-based management consulting firm, showcases a standout approach to engaging top corporate leaders by employing the above two steps. Corporate executives are busy people always short on time, are used to processing lots of information quickly, and get impatient when they feel like someone isn't getting to the point. Aligning with executives' perspective on time efficiency and straightforwardness, McKinsey has trained its employees to kick off the consulting sessions by directly offering concise bullet point recommendations. After these initial suggestions, consultants adapt their supporting details and analyses based on the flow of the conversation—an approach famously named as the *Pyramid Principle*. This method involves real-time information gathering and reasoning, presenting a pre-considered path while actively understanding the client's perspective to craft the most fitting strategies during discussions.

Perspective-taking is our best counter to physiological biases prevalent in our workplaces. Considering the enormous depth of perspective-taking as a topic, readers will have to dive-in into author's next book on perspective-taking.

Conclusion & Further Reading

"Fortunately for serious minds, a bias recognized is a bias sterilized." ~ Benjamin Haydon

After a class-action lawsuit against Xerox and others in 1973, when these companies were sued for unlawful discrimination in hiring minorities, a systematic process of addressing racial bias was introduced in corporate culture. Since then, the more visible biases at our workplace, related to race or diversity, have been recognized and their avoidance instilled into the collective consciousness of corporate employees through regular training. Though a lot more needs to happen, things seem to be improving since then, to the extent that we today see a lot of diversity in senior management positions and corporate boards across industries. But the same cannot be said for the more intrinsic hidden psychological biases that are at play in our office environments daily.

Unlike racial biases, there are no mandatory mass initiatives in the corporate world to counter psychological biases. The most we see are the efforts made through optional management courses, self-help books, and corporate talks. It can be safely assumed that everyone around us, including us, especially at the lower and mid-management levels, has flaws and inbuilt biases.

A workplace culture doesn't need to be toxic to have psychological biases play a major role in every aspect of our daily office life. Everyone in the office identifies with a specific tribe that influences their thoughts and beliefs. In almost all cases people don't even realize the extent to which their behaviors are biased due to psychological biases hidden very deep inside their consciousness.

The only solution seems to be a two-step approach of:

1. Self-awareness and
2. Perspective thinking.

We cannot rely on others and expect the next person we meet to be more aware and not ignorant about their own intrinsic biases. It is for our good that we work to pull ourselves out of ignorance and master the art of succeeding within the realities of a corporate environment. It's this realization that leads to making imperfect things work in tandem to the extent of achieving great results in our careers. Hence, it falls on individuals to make themselves aware of these possible biases they might face at the workplace.

Theory of Corporate Mind aims to bring forth my experiences from a decade-and-a-half long career in the tech corporate world. My focus is to help newcomers & mid-senior folks learn something early in their careers what I learned gradually over several years, which is:

"Humans, no matter how high in the corporate hierarchy, are not perfect creatures and thus expecting a flawless and perfect environment in a workplace is not realistic."

Having described and introduced the basic psychological flaws prevailing at our workplaces in this book, I intend to help the readers master the art of Perspective Thinking to counter workplace biases in my next series of books.

93

Please leave us reviews and stay tuned for more!

Scan this QR code to explore more on this topic –

Instagram: @PowerOfPerceptions

---------------------- X --------------------

References

1. Reference from chapter on Richard Nixon in book titled *"Leadership"* by Henry Kissinger.

2. Study titled *"When to Use Your Head and When to Use Your Heart: The Differential Value of Perspective-Taking Versus Empathy in Competitive Interactions"* by Debra Gilin, William W. Maddux, Jordan Carpenter, and Adam D. Galinsky.

3. Study titled *"Alternative Models of Price Behavior in Dyadic Negotiations: Market Prices, Reservation Prices, and Negotiator Aspirations"* by White Sally Blount, Valley Kathleen L., Bazerman Max H., Neale Margaret A., Peck Sharon R.

4. Study titled *"Smarter and Slower: Self-Other Merging and Stereotype Judgment/Behavior Dissociation Following Perspective-Taking"* by Adam D. Galinsky, Cynthia Wang and Gillian Ku.

5. Study titled *"Inclusion of Other in the Self Scale and the structure of interpersonal closeness"* by Arthur Aron, Elaine N. Aron, and Danny Smollan.

6. Study titled *"Confirmation Bias: A Ubiquitous Phenomenon in Many Guises"* by Raymond S. Nickerson.

7. Book titled *"Poor Economics"* by Abhijit Banerjee, Esther Duflo.

8. Study titled *"The Actor and the Observer: Divergent Perceptions of the causes of behavior"* by Edward E. Jones and Richard E. Nisbett.

9. Study titled *"Studies of independence and conformity"* by Solomon E. Asch.

10. Study titled *"Loss Aversion in Riskless Choice"* by Amos Tversky and Daniel Kahneman.

11. Article titled *"The Power of Small Wins"* by Teresa M. Amabile and Steven J. Kramer in Harvard Business Review.

12. Book titled *"The Man Who Lied to His Laptop: What We Can Learn About Ourselves from Our Machines"* by Clifford Nass and Corina Yen.

13. Study Titled *"Metacognitive Experiences in Consumer Judgment and Decision Making"* by Norbert Schwarz.